Introduction

A story that I heard many years ago as a student is one I have always treasured, not least because it highlights the uniqueness of the gift of mercy. The tale is told of a young French soldier who deserted Napoleon's army but who, within a matter of hours, was captured by his own troops. To discourage soldiers from abandoning their posts the penalty for desertion was death: there would be no trial, no defence, just a sure judgement. The runaway soldier's mother was Napoleon's principal cook, and when she heard what had happened she went to beg the great military commander to spare the life of her son. She went on her knees, pleading for mercy. Napoleon heard her plea but pointed out that because of the serious nature of the crime her son had committed he clearly did not deserve mercy.

"I know he doesn't deserve mercy," the mother answered. "It would not be mercy if he deserved it."

I don't know about this woman's culinary abilities, but wasn't she a good theologian? That is the point about mercy: nobody deserves it. Everyone deserves true justice; mercy, on the other hand, is sheer gift. Mercy cancels out wrongs and transgressions – not because a sparkling defence has been found or excusing causes have been skilfully argued – but because that is the considered response of the one who is grieved. Mercy does not suggest that the guilty are not guilty; it recognises the wrongdoing but does not demand

sat[...]
refl[...]
who[...]

In p[...] Jubilee Year of Mercy – beginning on 8 December 2015 (the Solemnity of the Immaculate Conception) and concluding on 20 November 2016 (the Solemnity of Jesus Christ, King of the Universe) – Pope Francis has given the Church a special time to celebrate the tender-heartedness of God. And a challenging time to reflect on how the Church and all of us can reflect this glorious characteristic of our bountiful God.

It is surely no coincidence that the Jubilee of Mercy falls in the liturgical cycle Year C, when we listen to Luke, whom Dante described as "the scribe of the gentleness of Christ." You can see how Edward Burne-Jones captured this insight beautifully in his stained-glass window of the evangelist. Luke will prove a gracious and stimulating companion throughout this year, not least with his parables of mercy such as the Good Samaritan and the Prodigal Son.

In Luke's Gospel, the gates of God's kingdom are open to all people of goodwill: God has no immigration policy. All Luke's heroes are outsiders and outcasts – the kind of people who are forgettable and overlooked in every other realm, but not in Jesus' kingdom. Luke knows about ambiguity in life: he knows that the good people in life are not always the correct people; he knows that decency and courtesy can come from the most unexpected quarters; he knows that kindness can flourish beyond the boundaries of religion. The heart of Luke's merciful Jesus is summarised in his mission statement:

"For the Son of Man came to seek out and to save the lost" (Luke 19:10).

In Pope Francis' Bull of Indiction of the Jubilee, *Misericordiae Vultus* (The Face of Mercy), he writes:

"The Church is commissioned to announce the mercy of God, the beating heart of the Gospel, which in its own way must penetrate the heart and mind of every person... It is absolutely essential for the Church and for the credibility of her message that she herself live and testify to mercy. Her language and her gestures must transmit mercy, so as to touch the hearts of all people and inspire them once more to find the road that leads to the Father" (MV, 12).

Pope Francis argues that the Church must not only plead for God's mercy but be a treasure house of mercy for all peoples. If Jesus our Lord is the face of the Father's mercy, so the Church must shine forth with that mercy to a waiting and wanting world. As Pope Francis emphasises:

"Wherever the Church is present, the mercy of the Father must be evident. In our parishes, communities, associations and movements, in a word, wherever there are Christians, everyone should find an oasis of mercy" (MV, 12).

But it might be true to say that mercy has become somewhat outdated in a world that seems more attentive to its rights and privileges than to the diminishing sense of kind-heartedness and forgiveness. For many people, mercy is a sign of feebleness of character or frailty of mind: one should insist, the conventional wisdom goes, on personal rights and propriety and entitlement. This conflict was beautifully explored by Shakespeare in the court scene of *The Merchant of Venice* where the complainant Shylock stubbornly insists on his rights in law. Portia, as judge, offers this counsel:

"Though justice be thy plea, consider this, That in the course of justice none of us Should see salvation: we do pray for mercy, And that same prayer doth teach us all to render The deeds of mercy"
(*The Merchant of Venice*, Act IV, scene i).

Shakespeare has managed in a few lines to summarise the beauty and challenge of God's mercy: the mercy of God, freely given, obliges us. Mercy is indivisible: one cannot demand it for oneself while withholding it from others. As Jesus ben Sirach noted:

"Forgive your neighbour the wrong he has done, and then your sins will be pardoned when you pray. Does anyone harbour anger against another, and expect healing from the Lord? If one has no mercy towards another like himself, can he then seek pardon for his own sins?" (Sirach 28:2-4).

It is Pope Francis' fond hope that we will use this Jubilee of Mercy as a year of grace to approach our merciful Father with confidence and accept the challenge of Jesus: "Be merciful, just as your Father is merciful" (Luke 6:36) – the motto for the Year of Mercy. We are challenged to adopt that mercy in our lifestyle by acting out the corporal and spiritual works of mercy. Pope Francis writes:

"It is my burning desire that, during this Jubilee, the Christian people may reflect on the *corporal and spiritual works of mercy*. It will be a way to reawaken our conscience, too often grown dull in the face of poverty. And let us enter more deeply into the heart of the Gospel where the poor have a special experience of God's mercy. Jesus introduces us to these works of mercy in his preaching so that we can know whether or not we are living as his disciples" (MV, 15).

As disciples of Jesus we are all tested by the quality of our mercy. In the apocalyptic vision of the Last Judgement, given to the disciples prior to his death, Jesus focuses attention on his continuing presence among those who are poor and needy (Matthew 25:31-46). It is as if Jesus deliberately turns his own followers away from an exclusive attraction to himself, away from a restricted focus on his own person, to look elsewhere to find him. In so doing, he challenges us to face the pain and loss endured by others, not to keep staring at him. He will be found where others suffer.

In the parable Jesus reveals his own profound respect for those who suffer in the midst of life. At the same time he hallows the many ordinary kindnesses of those who have never heard of him – the vast majority of humankind – and claims that the way of mercy is a way to the fullness of the kingdom.

There are many roads to God: mercy to the legion of those in need is one of the most sure.

I hope that everyone who reads these lines has a graced time during this Jubilee Year of Mercy, coming closer to our God who is rich in graciousness and mercy.

Denis McBride

Denis McBride C.Ss.R.
Publishing Director

The Corporal Works of Mercy

- ◆ Feed the hungry
- ◆ Give drink to the thirsty
- ◆ Clothe the naked
- ◆ Shelter the homeless
- ◆ Visit the sick
- ◆ Visit the imprisoned
- ◆ Bury the dead

The Spiritual Works of Mercy

- ◆ Admonish the sinner
- ◆ Instruct the ignorant
- ◆ Counsel the doubtful
- ◆ Comfort the sorrowful
- ◆ Bear wrongs patiently
- ◆ Forgive all injuries
- ◆ Pray for the living and the dead

DECEMBER

Beginning of the Year of Mercy

Our Jubilee Year begins on 8 December 2015. In *Misericordiae Vultus* Pope Francis wrote:

"I have chosen the date of 8 December because of its rich meaning in the recent history of the Church. In fact, I will open the Holy Door on the fiftieth anniversary of the closing of the Second Vatican Ecumenical Council... The Council Fathers strongly perceived, as a true breath of the Holy Spirit, a need to talk about God to men and women of their time in a more accessible way. The walls which too long had made the Church a kind of fortress were torn down and the time had come to proclaim the Gospel in a new way" (*Misericordiae Vultus*, 4).

When you think of the two great figures who dominate the beginnings of the Christian story, John the Baptist and Jesus, it is interesting to note that they made themselves easily accessible to all people by preaching their message out of doors rather than confining themselves to sacred space. John the Baptist preached in the wilderness, beside the banks of the River Jordan, attracting a legion of characters – like prostitutes and soldiers and tax collectors – who would never show their face in sacred space. You see Jesus preaching the Gospel in market-places, by the shores of the lake, on hillsides and in people's houses. Those who presided over the sacred space of the Temple not only objected to Jesus' teaching but were conspirators in his violent execution.

Many people feel ill at ease in sacred space today. Many have left. Do you think the Church limits her pastoral outreach to the world by confining herself too much to sacred space?

1

2

3

St Francis Xavier
Migrants' Day (England & Wales)

4

5

6	**13** SUNDAY
nd Sunday of Advent ble Sunday (England & Wales)	3rd Sunday of Advent
7	**14** MONDAY
nd Week of Advent Ambrose	3rd Week of Advent St John of the Cross
8	**15** TUESDAY
EGINNING OF THE YEAR OF MERCY e Immaculate Conception the Blessed Virgin Mary	
9	**16** WEDNESDAY
John Roberts (Wales)	
0	**17** THURSDAY
1	**18** FRIDAY
2	**19** SATURDAY

SUNDAY	20		27
	4th Sunday of Advent		The Holy Family of Jesus, Mary & Joseph

MONDAY	21		28
	4th Week of Advent		The Holy Innocents, Martyrs Bank Holiday

TUESDAY	22		29
			St Thomas à Becket (England)

WEDNESDAY	23		30

THURSDAY	24		31

James Tissot, *The Beatitudes* (detail)

FRIDAY	25
	The Nativity of the Lord Bank Holiday

SATURDAY	26
	St Stephen, the First Martyr

JANUARY 2016					
SUN	31	3	10	17	24
MON		4	11	18	25
TUES		5	12	19	26
WED		6	13	20	27
THUR		7	14	21	28
FRI	1	8	15	22	29
SAT	2	9	16	23	30

DECEMBER 2015

"Everyone thinks forgiveness is a lovely idea, until they have something to forgive."

C.S. Lewis

PRAYER

Out of the depths I cry to you, O Lord,
Lord, hear my voice!
O let your ears be attentive
to the voice of my pleading.

If you, O Lord, should mark our guilt,
Lord, who would survive?
But with you is found forgiveness:
for this we revere you.

Psalm 130:1-4

JANUARY 2016

Jesus' mission of mercy

Luke begins Jesus' public ministry with his return to Nazareth, his own home place. When he left home to travel south and meet John the Baptist, Jesus was known locally only as the son of Joseph the carpenter. When he returns, after his baptism by John and anointing in the Spirit, Jesus reveals a new identity to his people: the accomplished preacher and prophet. Will the locals accept him?

When Jesus goes into his local synagogue on the Sabbath as he usually did, this time he is invited to preach. He chooses a passage from Isaiah which gives a graceful summary of the programme of his new mission: to announce good news to the poor, proclaim liberty to captives and new sight to the blind; to free the oppressed and to proclaim a jubilee year of favour. His mission of mercy begins in his own home town.

Pope Francis comments on this scene: "A 'year of the Lord's favour' or 'mercy': this is what the Lord proclaimed and this is what we wish to live now. This Holy Year will bring to the fore the richness of Jesus' mission" (*Misericordiae Vultus*, 16).

Jesus' first mission, however, ends in disaster. While the locals' initial reaction is approval, they move quickly to rejection, insisting: "This is Joseph's son, surely?" They close out his message of mercy as they focus on the Jesus they know: they won't allow Jesus to become more than their frozen familiarity knows of him.

Jesus will always be much more than we can know of him; and he calls us beyond what we know of ourselves. Jesus' message will always call us beyond familiar boundaries, to a new generosity and mercy.

1

Mary, the Holy Mother of God
New Year Bank Holiday

2

Ss Basil & Gregory

	10 **SUNDAY**
he Epiphany of the Lord (England & Wales, Scotland) nd Sunday after the Nativity (Ireland)	The Baptism of the Lord
	11 **MONDAY**
ank Holiday (Scotland)	1st Week in Ordinary Time
	12 **TUESDAY**
	13 **WEDNESDAY**
e Epiphany of the Lord (Ireland)	St Kentigern (Scotland)
	14 **THURSDAY**
	15 **FRIDAY**
	16 **SATURDAY**

SUNDAY	**17** 2nd Sunday in Ordinary Time Peace Day (England & Wales)	**24** 3rd Sunday in Ordinary Time Education Day (England & Wales)
MONDAY	**18** 2nd Week in Ordinary Time Octave of Prayer for Christian Unity	**25** 3rd Week in Ordinary Time The Conversion of St Paul the Apostle
TUESDAY	**19**	**26** Ss Timothy and Titus, Bishops
WEDNESDAY	**20**	**27**
THURSDAY	**21** St Agnes	**28** St Thomas Aquinas
FRIDAY	**22**	**29**
SATURDAY	**23**	**30**

-th Sunday in Ordinary Time

James Tissot, *Jesus Unrolls the Book in the Synagogue* (detail)

JANUARY 2016

"I think we too are the people who, on the one hand, want to listen to Jesus, but on the other hand, at times, like to find a stick to beat others with, to condemn others. And Jesus has this message for us: mercy. I think – and I say it with humility – that this is the Lord's most powerful message: mercy."

Pope Francis,
The Church of Mercy

PRAYER

Have mercy on me, God, in your kindness.
In your compassion blot out my offence.
O wash me more and more from my guilt
And cleanse me from my sin.

Psalm 51:1-2

FEBRUARY 2016

SUN		7	14	21	28
MON	1	8	15	22	29
TUES	2	9	16	23	
WED	3	10	17	24	
THUR	4	11	18	25	
FRI	5	12	19	26	
SAT	6	13	20	27	

FEBRUARY 2016

The love that transfigures

An old cryptic Chinese saying observes, "You cannot transfigure yourself." I presume it means that something must happen to you, to make you clearly change for the better, so that now you look radiant, shining, and more alive. Something is showing through that wasn't showing through before. Your visible change leads people to wonder. When you walk into a room people notice a difference about you: some might ask, "Whatever happened to you?" The presumption is that something must have happened to you; that you did not organise this transformation yourself: something must have come over you.

In Luke's Gospel, the first narrative of Jesus' public ministry concludes with a strange incident: his own townspeople of Nazareth take Jesus from the local synagogue and then try to kill him by throwing him from a nearby hilltop. That violent rejection on a hilltop in Nazareth is dramatically reversed when Jesus later climbs to the higher hilltop of Mount Tabor and receives the loving acceptance of his Father.

The experience of disfiguration that Jesus undergoes at the hands of his own people can be dramatically juxtaposed with his experience of transfiguration on another mountain: on this summit he hears his name called in love, and that experience of fatherly approval radically changes him. Where the hills of Nazareth say no, Mount Tabor says yes; where Nazareth leads Jesus only to run away, Tabor leads him to set his face towards an ancient appointment in the city of Jerusalem.

Something happens to Jesus; something comes over him as he becomes radiant. What comes over him is the expression of his Father's love: it is the Father's expressed love that transfigures.

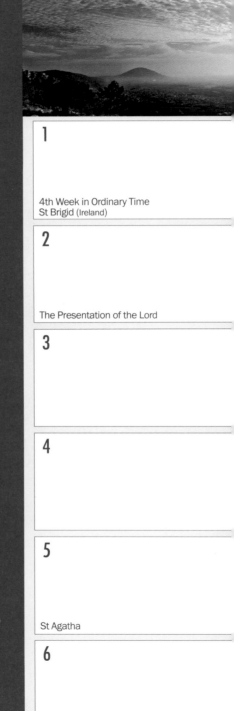

1

4th Week in Ordinary Time
St Brigid (Ireland)

2

The Presentation of the Lord

3

4

5

St Agatha

6

Ss Paul Miki & Companions

7

5th Sunday in Ordinary Time
Day for the Unemployed (England & Wales)

8

5th Week in Ordinary Time
Day for Victims of Trafficking

9

St Teilo (Wales)

10

Ash Wednesday

11

Our Lady of Lourdes
World Day for the Sick

12

13

14 SUNDAY

1st Sunday of Lent

15 MONDAY

1st Week of Lent

16 TUESDAY

17 WEDNESDAY

18 THURSDAY

19 FRIDAY

Lent Fast Day (England & Wales)

20 SATURDAY

| SUNDAY | 21 |
| | 2nd Sunday of Lent |

| | 28 |
| | 3rd Sunday of Lent |

MONDAY	22
	2nd Week of Lent
	The Chair of St Peter the Apostle

| | 29 |
| | 3rd Week of Lent |

| TUESDAY | 23 |
| | St Polycarp |

| WEDNESDAY | 24 |

| THURSDAY | 25 |

| FRIDAY | 26 |

| SATURDAY | 27 |

Mount Tabor in Lower Galilee

MARCH 2016					
SUN		6	13	20	27
MON		7	14	21	28
TUES	1	8	15	22	29
WED	2	9	16	23	30
THUR	3	10	17	24	31
FRI	4	11	18	25	
SAT	5	12	19	26	

FEBRUARY 2016

"Most woundedness remains hidden, lost inside forgotten silence. Indeed, in every life there is some wound that continues to weep secretly, even after years of attempted healing. Where woundedness can be refined into beauty a wonderful transfiguration takes place."

John O'Donohue

PRAYER

O Lord, grant thy compassion to go before us, thy compassion to come behind us; before us in undertaking, behind us in our ending. And what more shall I say, unless that thy will be done, who dost will that all should be saved. Thy will is our salvation, our glory and our joy.

Alcuin of York (735–804)

MARCH 2016

"Neither do I condemn you"

Imagine this scene. You have never managed to like her, nor she you. Whenever the two of you have met, the relationship has been tense, the conversation brittle, as you've exchanged unpleasantries effortlessly.

One day she says to you, "I have just made a thirty-day retreat under the Jesuits, and during all that time I have asked God for the grace to forgive people like you. On the twenty-ninth day God granted me the grace to forgive you in particular, since you have pained me in every bone of my body. I have come to tell you that I forgive you."

How does that make you feel? The way some people forgive is a new sin, since what is offered is not liberation from the past but a fresh way of demeaning people.

Throughout the pages of the Gospel Jesus never says, "I forgive you" – instead saying things like, "Your faith has saved you" or "Neither do I condemn you." Although Jesus offers forgiveness readily, he does not press or force the kindness tendered. Thus when he meets the sinful woman who had been caught in adultery, he does not take the side of the moral majority as they demand her death according to the Mosaic Law. He challenges the accusers to stop staring at the law book and have a look at their own book of life, in other words, to become self-reflective. Their self-reflection leads them away, leaving Jesus and the woman alone.

Jesus does not quiz her about her relationships or insist she confesses: his forgiveness liberates her and gives her new life. That is the nature of true forgiveness.

1

St David (Wales)

2

3

4

Women's World Day of Prayer

5

6

4th Sunday of Lent

7

4th Week of Lent
Ss Perpetua & Felicity

8

9

10

t John Ogilvie (Scotland)

11

12

13   SUNDAY

5th Sunday of Lent

14   MONDAY

5th Week of Lent

15   TUESDAY

16   WEDNESDAY

17   THURSDAY

St Patrick (England, Scotland, Ireland)
Bank Holiday (Ireland)

18   FRIDAY

19   SATURDAY

St Joseph, Spouse of the Blessed Virgin Mary

SUNDAY	20 Palm Sunday of the Passion of the Lord	27 Easter Sunday of the Resurrection of the Lord
MONDAY	21 Monday of Holy Week	28 Easter Monday Bank Holiday
TUESDAY	22 Tuesday of Holy Week	29 Easter Tuesday
WEDNESDAY	23 Wednesday of Holy Week	30 Easter Wednesday
THURSDAY	24 Thursday of the Lord's Supper (Maundy Thursday)	31 Easter Thursday
FRIDAY	25 Friday of the Passion of the Lord (Good Friday) Bank Holiday	
SATURDAY	26 Holy Saturday	

MARCH 2016

Guercino (Giovanni Francesco Barbieri), *Christ with the Woman Taken in Adultery* (detail)

"When faced with the gravity of sin, God responds with the fullness of mercy. Mercy will always be greater than any sin, and no one can place limits on the love of God who is ever ready to forgive."

Pope Francis,
Misericodiae Vultus, 3

APRIL 2016

SUN		3	10	17	24
MON		4	11	18	25
TUES		5	12	19	26
WED		6	13	20	27
THUR		7	14	21	28
FRI	1	8	15	22	29
SAT	2	9	16	23	30

PRAYER

Give thanks to the Lord, for he is good,
his love is everlasting!
Give thanks to the God of gods,
his love is everlasting!
Give thanks to the Lord of lords,
his love is everlasting!

Psalm 136:1-3

APRIL 2016

Paul: apostle of forgiveness

Before the war in Afghanistan that began in October 2001, news media around the world were carrying stories that the ruling party, the Taliban, were destroying anything from their pre-Islamic past, particularly images of the Buddha. We watched the Taliban destroy the great art of a modest religion. More recently we watched members of the so-called Islamic State destroy archaeological treasures in the ancient city of Palmyra.

That systematic destruction of images seems strange to modern ears; it is not as bad, however, as what Saul did at the beginning of his public career. Saul first appears as an accomplished persecutor not of images but of people, committed to destroying the followers of Jesus. Putting together religion and violence, Paul passionately believed in ethnic cleansing. As Luke tells us, "Saul worked for the total destruction of the Church" (Acts 8:3).

In spite of his violent past, Paul is chosen by Christ to be his apostle to the Gentiles. Paul goes to Jerusalem to share his experience with the apostles, but he stayed for only fifteen days. Luke tells us why: when Paul arrived "he tried to join the disciples, but they were afraid of him; they could not believe he really was a disciple" (Acts 9:26).

Unsurprisingly, Paul has real trouble in being accepted by the people he was persecuting; but he perseveres. As his new vocation began in the experience of the Lord's mercy, so that experience will dominate his life and thinking: "Bear with one another; forgive each other as soon as a quarrel begins. The Lord has forgiven you; now you must do the same" (Colossians 3:13).

For Paul, the experience of the Lord's mercy obliges us: what we have received freely we should give freely.

1

Easter Friday

2

Easter Saturday

3

2nd Sunday of Easter
Divine Mercy Sunday

10   SUNDAY

3rd Sunday of Easter

4

The Annunciation of the Lord
2nd Week of Easter

11   MONDAY

3rd Week of Easter
St Stanislaus

5

12   TUESDAY

6

13   WEDNESDAY

7

St John Baptist de la Salle

14   THURSDAY

8

15   FRIDAY

9

16   SATURDAY

SUNDAY 17	24
4th Sunday of Easter World Day of Prayer for Vocations	5th Sunday of Easter
MONDAY 18	25
4th Week of Easter	5th Week of Easter St Mark, Evangelist
TUESDAY 19	26
WEDNESDAY 20	27
St Bueno (Wales)	
THURSDAY 21	28
FRIDAY 22	29
	St Catherine of Siena
SATURDAY 23	30
St George (England)	

APRIL 2016

El Greco, *Saint Paul* (detail)

"*Our prayer also extends to the saints and the blessed ones who made divine mercy their mission in life. I am especially thinking of the great apostle of mercy, Saint Faustina Kowalska. May she, who was called to enter the depths of divine mercy, intercede for and obtain for us the grace of living and walking always according to the mercy of God and with an unwavering trust in his love.*"

Pope Francis,
Misericordiae Vultus, 24

MAY 2016

SUN	1	8	15	22	29
MON	2	9	16	23	30
TUES	3	10	17	24	31
WED	4	11	18	25	
THUR	5	12	19	26	
FRI	6	13	20	27	
SAT	7	14	21	28	

PRAYER

Forgive us our trespasses,
as we forgive those who trespass against us,
and lead us not into temptation,
but deliver us from evil.

MAY 2016

Mary, Mother of Mercy

If you walk into any Catholic church anywhere, usually you don't have to hunt to find some shrine erected in honour of Mary, the Mother of God. To many non-Catholic people, Catholics used to be identified popularly as the ones who ate fish on Fridays and had missals bulging with devotions to Our Lady. Catholics were different, somehow. You could watch them taking to the streets in May in glittering processions, carrying statues, banners, candles, rosaries, hymn sheets – all dressed in their Sunday best and singing hymns to the Queen of Heaven, the ocean star. And apart from the decked-out altar boys, they all looked as if they were having a good time.

In announcing the Jubilee Year of Mercy Pope Francis wrote:

"Chosen to be the Mother of the Son of God, Mary... treasured divine mercy in her heart in perfect harmony with her Son Jesus. Her hymn of praise, sung at the threshold of the home of Elizabeth, was dedicated to the mercy of God which extends from 'generation to generation'" (*Misericordiae Vultus*, 24).

One of the most beautiful icons of Mary, and probably the most popular in the Western world, is known as *Our Mother of Perpetual Succour*. It dates back to the fifteenth century in Crete. It was venerated in Rome from 1499 and eventually installed in the Church of St Alphonsus in Rome. In 1866, Pope Pius IX made the Redemptorists the custodians of the icon, challenging the Congregation to make her known, and this year we celebrate the 150th anniversary of that charge. We venerate Mary as the lowly servant, made great by the choice of God, and the Mother of Mercy whom all can approach with confidence.

1

6th Sunday of Easter

2

6th Week of Easter
St Athanasius
Bank Holiday

3

Ss Philip and James, Apostles

4

The English Martyrs (England)

5

The Ascension of the Lord (Scotland)
St Asaph (Wales)

6

7

8 The Ascension of the Lord (England & Wales, Ireland) 7th Sunday of Easter World Communications Day	15 Pentecost Sunday	SUNDAY
9 7th Week of Easter	16 7th Week in Ordinary Time St Brendan (Ireland)	MONDAY
10	17	TUESDAY
11	18	WEDNESDAY
12	19	THURSDAY
13	20	FRIDAY
14 St Matthias, Apostle	21	SATURDAY

SUNDAY 22

The Most Holy Trinity

SUNDAY 29

The Most Holy Body and Blood of Christ
(Corpus Christi) (England & Wales, Scotland)

MONDAY 23

8th Week in Ordinary Time

MONDAY 30

9th Week in Ordinary Time
Spring Bank Holiday

TUESDAY 24

TUESDAY 31

The Visitation of the Blessed Virgin Mary
Day for Life (Scotland)

WEDNESDAY 25

St Bede the Venerable (England)

THURSDAY 26

The Most Holy Body and Blood of Christ
(Corpus Christi) (Ireland)
St Philip Neri

FRIDAY 27

St Augustine of Canterbury (England)

SATURDAY 28

Icon: *Our Mother of Perpetual Succour* (detail)

MAY 2016

> *"Had Mary been filled with reason*
> *there'd have been no room for the child."*
>
> **Madeleine L'Engle**

JUNE 2016

	SUN	MON	TUES	WED	THUR	FRI	SAT
SUN		5	12	19	26		

SUN		5	12	19	26
MON		6	13	20	27
TUES		7	14	21	28
WED	1	8	15	22	29
THUR	2	9	16	23	30
FRI	3	10	17	24	
SAT	4	11	18	25	

PRAYER

My soul proclaims the greatness
of the Lord
and my spirit exults in God my
saviour;
because he has looked upon his
lowly handmaid.
Yes, from this day forward all
generations will call me blessed,
for the Almighty has done great
things for me.

Luke 1:46-48

JUNE 2016

Barnabas: apostle of encouragement

The evangelist Luke describes Barnabas as a "good man, full of the Holy Spirit and of faith" whose encouragement resulted in many people persevering in their faith. His real name was Joseph, from Cyprus, but such was his nature that he received the nickname Barnabas, which means "son of encouragement".

When Paul was exiled from Jerusalem back home to Tarsus, he could have disappeared for ever. But one man encouraged Paul in his new life and decided to sponsor him. Barnabas had been appointed to superintend the Church in Antioch, the capital of Syria. He sought out Paul and invited him to help him: it is while both of them are ministering in Antioch that the followers of Christ were first known as "Christians".

Paul and Barnabas travelled widely together: Luke tells us, "They put fresh heart into the disciples encouraging them to persevere in the faith" (Acts 14:22). Paul extended to others the encouragement he had received from Barnabas. For Barnabas recognised something in Paul that no other apostle perceived: he saw beyond the face of the persecutor into the heart of a man who was struggling to be an apostle.

Barnabas lives up to his name by helping Paul live up to his new name, apostle of Christ. By his encouragement Barnabas actually gives shape to Paul's life. He promotes the best in Paul; he assists the possible; he invests his time and love and energy in the person Paul can become. That is encouragement. We can all bless God for the people who have invested in us, who have encouraged us to be who we are. And we all need to pray that when the time comes, we too can be a Barnabas.

1

St Justin

2

3

The Most Sacred Heart of Jesus
Ss Charles Lwanga & Companions

4

The Immaculate Heart of the Blessed Virgin Ma

5

10th Sunday in Ordinary Time

12   SUNDAY

11th Sunday in Ordinary Time

6

10th Week in Ordinary Time

13   MONDAY

11th Week in Ordinary Time
St Anthony of Padua

7   TUESDAY

14

8   WEDNESDAY

15

9

St Columba (Colum Cille) (Ireland & Scotland)

16   THURSDAY

10

17   FRIDAY

11

St Barnabas, Apostle

18   SATURDAY

SUNDAY 19	**26**
12th Sunday in Ordinary Time	13th Sunday in Ordinary Time

MONDAY 20	**27**
12th Week in Ordinary Time St Alban (England) Ss Alban, Julius & Aaron (Wales)	13th Week in Ordinary Time

TUESDAY 21	**28**
St Aloysius Gonzaga	St Irenaeus

WEDNESDAY 22	**29**
Ss John Fisher & Thomas More (England)	Ss Peter and Paul, Apostles

THURSDAY 23	**30**

FRIDAY 24
The Nativity of St John the Baptist

SATURDAY 25

JUNE 2016

> "The Latin word misericordia, *according to its original sense, means to have one's heart* (cor) *with the poor* (miseri) *or to have a heart for the poor. It means to have a merciful heart.*"

Cardinal Walter Kasper

Richard Maidwell C.Ss.R., *Saints Barnabas and Paul* (detail)

JULY 2016

SUN		3	10	17	24	31
MON		4	11	18	25	
TUES		5	12	19	26	
WED		6	13	20	27	
THUR		7	14	21	28	
FRI	1	8	15	22	29	
SAT	2	9	16	23	30	

PRAYER

Remember in your mercy, Lord, the Church throughout the world. Heal its divisions, restore its unity, empower its witness, so that it might become the instrument of your purpose for the healing of the nations. Let it be a voice of encouragement to all who are disheartened and crushed. This we ask through our redeemer, Jesus Christ.

JULY 2016

The Good Samaritan

This great parable of mercy is one of the most challenging stories in the Gospels, where Jesus takes his own people's favourite enemy – the Samaritans – and turns one of them into a teacher and merciful hero. In the parable Jesus challenges his listeners to think again about those whose personal or social identities they deeply despise, those people who are rejected not because of their behaviour but because of institutionalised prejudice against them.

Being part of a particular group, social or religious or political, can enlarge our world, heighten our sense of belonging and help us form our own identity. One of the principal ways any group defines its identity is by asserting its difference from other groups: that pride in difference shows itself in flags and badges, beliefs and attitudes, rituals and traditions. Whatever the nature of the group – a tribe, a religion, a nationality, a political party – loyalty within the group can foster the growth of its members. Sometimes, however, the price for intense loyalty is hostility to outsiders, to those who don't belong to the group.

We know from our own experience the weight of inherited hostility against people who belong to the wrong crowd, an outlook that is often supported by a magical confidence in one's own crowd. We know that to accept some people in their difference is not only an act of love but also an act of defiance against the bigotry that sometimes passes for religion. Jesus tells us that we must be disloyal to those who would educate our hate. If religion needs hate to nurture it, who needs that kind of religion? Jesus comes to challenge our hate and promote our mercy.

1

St Oliver Plunkett (Ireland)

2

3

14th Sunday in Ordinary Time
St Thomas, Apostle

10   SUNDAY

15th Sunday in Ordinary Time
Sea Sunday

4

14th Week in Ordinary Time

11   MONDAY

15th Week in Ordinary Time
St Benedict

5

12   TUESDAY

St John Jones (Wales)

6

13   WEDNESDAY

7

14   THURSDAY

8

15   FRIDAY

St Bonaventure

9

Our Lady of Aberdeen (Scotland)

16   SATURDAY

Our Lady of Mount Carmel

SUNDAY	17	24
	16th Sunday in Ordinary Time	17th Sunday in Ordinary Time
MONDAY	18	25
	16th Week in Ordinary Time	17th Week in Ordinary Time St James, Apostle
TUESDAY	19	26
		Ss Joachim & Anne
WEDNESDAY	20	27
THURSDAY	21	28
FRIDAY	22	29
	St Mary Magdalene	St Martha
SATURDAY	23	30
	St Bridget	

31

18th Sunday in Ordinary Time
Day for Life (England & Wales)

"Mercy is the very foundation of the Church's life. All her pastoral activity should be caught up in the tenderness she makes present to believers; nothing in her preaching and in her witness to the world can be lacking in mercy. The Church's very credibility is seen in how much she shows merciful and compassionate love."

Pope Francis,
Misericordiae Vultus, 10

Vincent van Gogh, *The Good Samaritan* (detail)

AUGUST 2016					
SUN		7	14	21	28
MON	1	8	15	22	29
TUES	2	9	16	23	30
WED	3	10	17	24	31
THUR	4	11	18	25	
FRI	5	12	19	26	
SAT	6	12	20	27	

PRAYER

My dearest Lord,
be thou a bright flame before me,
be thou a guiding star above me,
be thou a smooth path beneath me,
be thou a kindly shepherd behind me,
today and for evermore.

AUGUST 2016

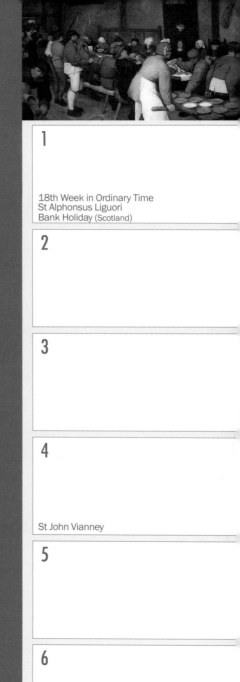

Who to invite to dinner?

When attending a wedding reception, many people worry about the seating arrangements at table, and fuss about who they will be landed next to at dinner. Some people check the seating arrangement and then make their own discreet exchange of name cards before the dinner begins, to assure themselves they can survive the lengthy meal in reasonable company.

Jesus' idea of an interesting dinner party is, however, most people's social nightmare: when you enter the dining room there are no relatives or friends in sight, only a gathering of "the poor, the crippled, the lame, the blind" (Luke 14:13). God is the eccentric host whose delight is to feast those who are always overlooked in a society that scrambles for honour. Welcome, please sit down!

The guest list might include the old lady in the moth-eaten coat who carries her kingdom in plastic bags; those who nightly inhabit the entrance enclosure to shops, sleeping in flattened cardboard boxes; blind people who have to feel for the warmth of a fire they cannot see; the lonely hearts who are never invited anywhere. These are the ones who are led to the seats of honour in the kingdom: the little people who cannot return the invitations and are hungry for the food and the company that table fellowship can bring. Jesus has a credo that hugs these people into importance.

Jesus keeps God's preference for the little people at the forefront of his teaching. He has the kind of love that sees beyond appearances, the kind of love that pierces disguises, the kind of love that calls people out of the shadows. His love dignifies people; he asks that our love does no less.

1

18th Week in Ordinary Time
St Alphonsus Liguori
Bank Holiday (Scotland)

2

3

4

St John Vianney

5

6

The Transfiguration of the Lord

7	14	**SUNDAY**
19th Sunday in Ordinary Time	20th Sunday in Ordinary Time The Assumption of the Blessed Virgin Mary (E&W)	

8	15	**MONDAY**
19th Week in Ordinary Time St Dominic	20th Week in Ordinary Time The Assumption of the Blessed Virgin Mary (S&I)	

9	16	**TUESDAY**
St Teresa Benedicta of the Cross		

10	17	**WEDNESDAY**
St Lawrence, Deacon and Martyr		

11	18	**THURSDAY**
St Clare		

12	19	**FRIDAY**

13	20	**SATURDAY**
	St Bernard	

| SUNDAY | 21 | 28 |

21st Sunday in Ordinary Time

22nd Sunday in Ordinary Time

MONDAY 22 **29**

21st Week in Ordinary Time
The Queenship of the Blessed Virgin Mary

22nd Week in Ordinary Time
The Passion of St John the Baptist
Summer Bank Holiday (England & Wales)

TUESDAY 23 **30**

WEDNESDAY 24 **31**

St Bartholomew, Apostle

THURSDAY 25

FRIDAY 26

St Ninian (Scotland)
St David Lewis (Wales)

Pieter Brueghel the Elder, *Peasant Wedding Feast* (detail)

SATURDAY 27

St Monica

SEPTEMBER 2016					
SUN		4	11	18	25
MON		5	12	19	26
TUES		6	13	20	27
WED		7	14	21	28
THUR	1	8	15	22	29
FRI	2	9	16	23	30
SAT	3	10	17	24	

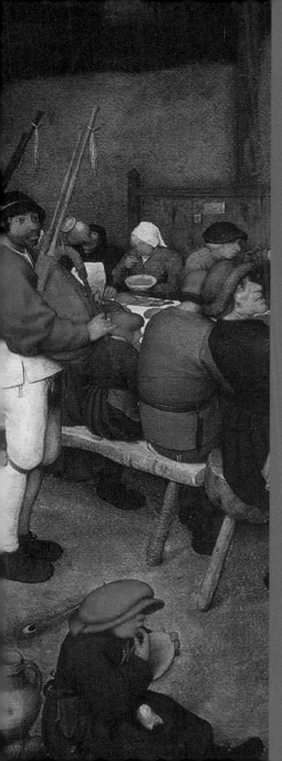

"This is why I want a Church which is poor and for the poor. They have much to teach us. Not only do they share in the sensus fidei, but in their difficulties they know the suffering Christ. We need to let ourselves be evangelised by them."

Pope Francis,
The Church of Mercy

PRAYER

We beg you, Lord, to help us and defend us. Deliver the oppressed, pity the insignificant, show yourself to the needy, heal the sick, feed the hungry. May every nation come to know that you alone are God.

St Clement of Rome

SEPTEMBER 2016

The supreme parable of mercy

The Prodigal Son is probably the best loved of Jesus' parables, not least because it explores two different reactions in the family to the return of the lost son and brother. The father has his reconciliation with his son in public, where everyone can witness how he accepts back his errant son. He makes no demand for a detailed account of what has gone wrong. It is worth noting that the father does not speak a word to his son; he doesn't need to. His language is spoken through his body: he sees, he runs, he gathers his son in his arms; he kisses him tenderly. You don't listen to this father welcome his son; you watch him: this is reconciliation through touch.

The father runs a second time, this time to his elder son, hoping he might join them in the family feast. The elder son lives in his own enclosed world of self-righteousness; he is skilled at reconstructing past wrongs; his arithmetic is impeccable, but his hard work has made him hard-hearted. One is reminded of a thought by Yeats: "Too long a sacrifice / Can make a stone of the heart."

The father does not allow his son's bitter resentment to change his own perspective; rather, he remains steadfastly gracious to both his sons. In effect the father tells his elder son that he has become a slave for something that is already in his keep – his inheritance has not been altered by his father's generosity to the younger son.

The father remains stubbornly gracious to both sons, offering us the good news that no matter what we have done, we can always return to our gracious Lord.

1

2

3

St Gregory the Great (England)

4		11	SUNDAY
3rd Sunday in Ordinary Time		24th Sunday in Ordinary Time Racial Justice Day (England & Wales)	

5		12	MONDAY
3rd Week in Ordinary Time		24th Week in Ordinary Time The Most Holy Name of Mary	

6		13	TUESDAY
		St John Chrysostom	

7		14	WEDNESDAY
		The Exaltation of the Holy Cross	

8		15	THURSDAY
The Nativity of the Blessed Virgin Mary		Our Lady of Sorrows	

9		16	FRIDAY
		Ss Cornelius & Cyprian St Ninian (Scotland)	

10		17	SATURDAY

SUNDAY 18	25
25th Sunday in Ordinary Time Home Mission Day (England & Wales)	26th Sunday in Ordinary Time

MONDAY 19	26
25th Week in Ordinary Time	26th Week in Ordinary Time

TUESDAY 20	27
Ss Andrew Kim Tae-gon, Paul Chong Ha-Song & Companions	St Vincent de Paul

WEDNESDAY 21	28
St Matthew, Apostle and Evangelist	

THURSDAY 22	29
	Ss Michael, Gabriel and Raphael, Archangels

FRIDAY 23	30
St Pio of Pietrelcina	St Jerome

SATURDAY 24	
Our Lady of Walsingham (England)	

SEPTEMBER 2016

Bartolomé Murillo, *The Return of the Prodigal Son* (detail)

"In the parables devoted to mercy... God is always presented as full of joy, especially when he pardons. In them we find the core of the Gospel and of our faith, because mercy is presented as a force that overcomes everything, filling the heart with love and bringing consolation through pardon."

Pope Francis,
Misericordiae Vultus, 9

PRAYER

When Israel was a child I loved him,
and I called my son out of Egypt.

I took them in my arms...
I led them with reins of kindness,
with leading-strings of love.
I was like someone who lifts an infant
close against his cheek;
stooping down to him I gave him his food.

Hosea 11:1. 3-4

OCTOBER 2016

SUN		2	9	16	23	30
MON		3	10	17	24	31
TUES		4	11	18	25	
WED		5	12	19	26	
THUR		6	13	20	27	
FRI		7	14	21	28	
SAT	1	8	15	22	29	

OCTOBER 2016

A woman demands justice

When Jesus wants to teach his disciples about persistence in prayer he uses an unusual heroine in the desperate widow who keeps on demanding justice. She takes on the weight of the legal system and, despite the unlikelihood of a positive outcome, refuses to accept the fate assigned to her by her social position or by the obduracy of the judge. She refuses to play the role of the silent, mourning widow who suffers her loss without protest; she refuses to lead her life off-stage, unseen and unacknowledged.

Instead, she enters the drama and shamelessly dominates the centre of the stage, effectively stealing the scene from the main character, the judge. She stays centre-stage, taking on the world of patriarchal power until she eventually succeeds in winning recognition for who she is: a poor widow who stays hungry for justice until she receives what is her right. We, who watch her, can only applaud such a spirited performance.

In the Christian tradition the widow is our teacher. She teaches us not to be overawed by the powerful who have the last word, not to give permission to the corrupt to rule our lives. She teaches us to be equal to our desperation by being stubborn in our commitment; she challenges us to invest our time and energy in what we believe to be right, to face up to formidable opposition in the war of nerves, even if we have to batter down social boundaries that would keep us from our objective. She teaches us the art of protest. And she leaves behind her the echo of her cry:

"Stay crying for justice until you exhaust the mighty into justice."

1

St Thérèse of Lisieux

2	**9** SUNDAY
7th Sunday in Ordinary Time ay for Life (Ireland)	28th Sunday in Ordinary Time
3	**10** MONDAY
7th Week in Ordinary Time	28th Week in Ordinary Time
4	**11** TUESDAY
Francis of Assisi	
5	**12** WEDNESDAY
6	**13** THURSDAY
7	**14** FRIDAY
ur Lady of the Rosary arvest Fast Day (England & Wales)	
8	**15** SATURDAY
	St Teresa of Avila

SUNDAY	16 29 Sunday in Ordinary Time	23 30th Sunday in Ordinary Time World Mission Day
MONDAY	17 29th Week in Ordinary Time St Ignatius of Antioch	24 30th Week in Ordinary Time
TUESDAY	18 St Luke, Evangelist	25 Six Welsh Martyrs & Companions (Wales)
WEDNESDAY	19	26
THURSDAY	20	27
FRIDAY	21	28 Ss Simon and Jude, Apostles
SATURDAY	22	29

0

1st Sunday in Ordinary Time

1

1st Week in Ordinary Time

OCTOBER 2016

John Everett Millais, *Parable of the Unjust Judge* (detail)

NOVEMBER 2016					
SUN		6	13	20	27
MON		7	14	21	28
TUES	1	8	15	22	29
WED	2	9	16	23	30
THUR	3	10	17	24	
FRI	4	11	18	25	
SAT	5	12	19	26	

PRAYER

O Lord, we pray that you will hasten the time when no people will live in contentment while they know their neighbours live in need. Inspire in all of us the sensitivity that we are not our own but yours and our neighbours'. This we ask for the sake of the one who prayed that we might all be one in him.

NOVEMBER 2016

Praying for the dead

The Church has always taught that our charity should not be limited to the living. Charity and prayer have the power to cross the last boundary – death itself – and throughout November we traditionally pray for the dead and keep their memory alive. We keep a pledge not to forget: not to forget those who have gone before us, those who await completion, those who can still be touched by the charity that finds its voice in prayer.

Probably all of us have experienced the death of someone we love. No matter how prepared we are for their death, their departure is always an acutely felt loss, not a vague symptom. Everything that previously seemed important now seems suddenly frivolous beside the stark realness of a large absence. Because we love people, we miss them when they die. And we can feel disabled inside for a long time, long after everyone else believes we have reached "closure". With those we love, most of us do not want to reach closure: our unbroken experience of loss is a measure of the intensity of our love.

We believe that Jesus is Lord not only of the living but of the dead: that faith gives substance to our hope. So this month, as we bring the Jubilee Year of Mercy to a close, we pray for those we have known and those we never knew. Our prayers embrace all those who have died lonely deaths in the absence of love and support. When we die we will be encouraged by the charity of the Christian community which will remember us in prayer. We keep that tradition of charity alive when we pray for the dead.

1

All Saints

2

The Commemoration of All the Faithful Departe (All Souls' Day)

3

4

St Charles Borromeo

5

6 2nd Sunday in Ordinary Time	13 33rd Sunday in Ordinary Time Remembrance Day	SUNDAY
7 2nd Week in Ordinary Time	14 33rd Week in Ordinary Time	MONDAY
8 l Saints of Wales (Wales)	15	TUESDAY
9 e Dediication of the Lateran Basilica	16 St Margaret (Scotland)	WEDNESDAY
0 Leo the Great	17	THURSDAY
1 Martin of Tours	18	FRIDAY
2 Josaphat	19	SATURDAY

SUNDAY 20

CLOSE OF THE YEAR OF MERCY
Our Lord Jesus Christ, King of the Universe

27

YEAR A
1st Sunday of Advent

MONDAY 21

Last Week in Ordinary Time
The Presentation of the Blessed Virgin Mary

28

1st Week of Advent

TUESDAY 22

St Cecilia

29

WEDNESDAY 23

St Columban (Ireland)

30

St Andrew, Apostle
Bank Holiday (Scotland)

THURSDAY 24

St Andrew Dung-Lac & Companions

Giotto di Bondone, *Lamentation* (deta

FRIDAY 25

SATURDAY 26

DECEMBER 2016					
SUN		4	11	20	25
MON		5	12	19	26
TUES		6	13	20	27
WED		7	14	21	28
THUR	1	8	15	22	29
FRI	2	9	16	23	30
SAT	3	10	17	24	31

NOVEMBER 2016

"If Job's sons were purified by their father's sacrifice, why should we doubt that our offerings for the dead bring them some consolation? Let us not hesitate to help those who have died and to offer our prayers for them."

St John Chrysostom

PRAYER

*This earth is for us a battlefield
where we have to fight and conquer
in order to be saved.
But when we reach heaven
our state is changed.
There will be no more toil, but rest;
no more fear, but security;
no more sadness or weariness,
but gladness and joy eternal.*

St Alphonsus Liguori

DECEMBER 2016

Living a life of mercy

With the closing of the Jubilee Year of Mercy, we aim not to leave mercy behind us with a sigh of relief so we can return to ordinary time and our usual hesitant regard for others. Our real challenge is to live a life of mercy: to shelter those in need of kindness, to reach out to those enclosed in hurt, to forgive those hedged in by past mistakes.

As we move into a new liturgical year with Matthew as our guide, we will hear Jesus speak about himself as the gentle-hearted teacher:

"Come to me, all you who labour and are overburdened and I will give you rest. Shoulder my yoke and learn from me, for I am gentle and humble in heart, and you will find rest for your souls. Yes, my yoke is easy and my burden light" (Matthew 11:28-30).

Jesus has a merciful word for all who are bowed down by an interpretation of the Law that leaves them mugged into senselessness. While Jesus has no intention of doing away with the Law, he refuses to support the lawyers who spend their time manufacturing new burdens for broken people. Jesus offers all those who struggle an invitation, "Come to me... learn from me... and you will find rest for your souls." Jesus makes himself the centre of his own teaching.

God has chosen Jesus to be the one who embodies the fullness of revelation and the new Law of Christ, a law characterised by mercy. As that mercy governs the heart of Jesus, it should govern our hearts as his disciples. The year of mercy is always ahead of us, not behind us.

1

2

3

St Francis Xavier

4		11	SUNDAY
nd Sunday of Advent		3rd Sunday of Advent	

5		12	MONDAY
nd Week of Advent		3rd Week of Advent	

6		13	TUESDAY
		St Lucy	

7		14	WEDNESDAY
Ambrose		St John of the Cross	

8		15	THURSDAY
e Immaculate Conception the Blessed Virgin Mary			

9		16	FRIDAY

0		17	SATURDAY

SUNDAY 18	25
4th Sunday of Advent	The Nativity of the Lord Bank Holiday
MONDAY 19	26
4th Week of Advent	St Stephen, the First Martyr Boxing Day
TUESDAY 20	27
	St John, Apostle and Evangelist Bank Holiday
WEDNESDAY 21	28
	The Holy Innocents, Martyrs
THURSDAY 22	29
	St Thomas à Becket (England)
FRIDAY 23	30
	The Holy Family of Jesus, Mary and Joseph
SATURDAY 24	31

DECEMBER 2016

Richard Maidwell C.Ss.R., *Christ the Teacher* (detail)

*"But mercy is above this
sceptred sway;
It is enthronèd in the hearts
of kings,
It is an attribute to God
himself;
And earthly power doth then
show likest God's
When mercy seasons
justice."*

William Shakespeare,
The Merchant of Venice, Act IV, scene i

PRAYER

*You are merciful to all, because you
are almighty, you overlook people's
sins, so that they can repent. Yes,
you love everything that exists,
and nothing that you have made
disgusts you, since, if you had hated
something, you would not have
made it... No, you spare all, since all
is yours, Lord, lover of life!*

Wisdom 11: 23-24. 26

JANUARY 2017

SUN	1	8	15	22	29
MON	2	9	16	23	30
TUES	3	10	17	24	31
WED	4	11	18	25	
THUR	5	12	19	26	
FRI	6	13	20	27	
SAT	7	14	21	28	

CONTACTS

Name	Telephone	Email

NOTABLE DATES 2017

Mary, the Holy Mother of God	Sunday 1 January
Bank Holiday	Monday 2 January
Epiphany of the Lord	Friday 6 January (Ireland) Sunday 8 January (E&W,S)
Ash Wednesday	Wednesday 1 March
Good Friday (Public Holiday)	Friday 14 April
Easter Sunday	Sunday 16 April
Easter Monday (Bank Holiday–not Scotland)	Monday 17 April
May Bank Holiday	Monday 1 May
Spring Bank Holiday (UK)	Monday 29 May
Pentecost Sunday	Sunday 4 June
June Bank Holiday (Ireland)	Monday 5 June
The Most Holy Trinity	Sunday 11 June
Corpus Christi	Thursday 15 June (Scotland) Sunday 18 June (E&W)
Ss Peter and Paul	Thursday 29 June
Summer Bank Holiday (Scotland)	Monday 7 August
Assumption of the BVM	Tuesday 15 August
Summer Bank Holiday (UK, except Scotland)	Monday 28 August
World Mission Sunday	Sunday 22 October
October Bank Holiday (Ireland)	Monday 30 October
All Saints	Wednesday 1 November
All Souls	Thursday 2 November
Christ the King	Sunday 26 November
First Sunday of Advent	Sunday 3 December
Immaculate Conception of the BVM	Friday 8 December
Christmas Day	Monday 25 December
Boxing Day Holiday	Tuesday 26 December
Holy Family	Sunday 31 December

PLANNING  2017

JANUARY

FEBRUARY

MARCH

APRIL

PLANNING  2017

MAY

JUNE

JULY

AUGUST

PLANNING  2017

SEPTEMBER

OCTOBER

NOVEMBER

DECEMBER